This book is dedicated to my nephews and nieces:
Jonathan, Garren, Savannah and Katie

I want you each to know that you are the inspiration for this book. Your aunt and I are truly blessed to have you in our lives. Thank you for simply being you.

A couple of you are too young to read this book right now, much less understand the concepts in it. But don't you worry, when the time comes, I will be here, ready to teach you everything you need to know about investing for your retirement.

Until then, just have fun being a kid. You will have plenty of time to be an adult. Life passes by quickly, so enjoy the small things in life, sing and dance like no one is watching and always be ready to help a friend in need.

For you two old enough to read this book and understand the concepts in it, I can't wait to get your honest feedback. I am so proud of the men you have turned into and I am looking forward to seeing what you do in your lives. Always remember that you live in the greatest country in the world. And the only thing stopping you from getting what you want out of life…is you.

Love You Always,

Uncle Butch

Graphic Designer: Alonza Carter
Cartercreationsgd@gmail.com

Cover Photo:

Licensed Through Canva
JTP-2588865 ID-CPA4vXev4pOqrOliFDSqTr
The people in the photo are paid actors

Editors:

Wanda Kerschbaum
Marla Barbour
Kelli Mauldin

TABLE OF CONTENTS

LITTLE LUCIE HIT THE JACKPOT!

Back in 2004, my friend and mentor told me he had just set up a ROTH IRA for his newborn granddaughter, Lucie. I was blown away by this idea!

Simply because her grandfather was an astute investor, little Lucie already had her very own retirement account that would be able to grow for a **Full 65 Years... TAX FREE!**

Her grandfather told me his plan was to contribute a minimum of $1,000 into her ROTH IRA each and every year until she reaches adulthood. Then he said he planned on turning it over to her so she can continue contributing into it and managing the account herself until she reaches retirement age.

I couldn't believe what I was hearing! I immediately knew this simple concept was ingenious and little Lucie had just hit the jackpot!

I went home that day with these questions in mind:

1. Assuming $1,000 per year is invested in Lucie's retirement account for the next 65 years and that account grows (compounds) at an average annual rate of 9%, how much would her retirement account be worth when she turned 65?

$2,998,288.47

2. How much can she expect to be able to live on each and every year after she reaches retirement age?

$269,845.96

This is what these calculations told me:

If Lucie does nothing more than take over her ROTH IRA and continues to invest a mere $1,000 per year into it until she is 65 years old and if she can realize an average annual growth rate of 9%... **she will be able to live on nearly $270,000 per year... TAX FREE... for the rest of her life... no matter how long she lives! And then she can pass that $2,998,288.47 on to her loved ones!**

That's when I realized that my mentor was building himself a real Legacy and creating GENERATIONAL WEALTH for his family!

I couldn't believe it! Little Lucie had REALLY hit the jackpot! **BUT SO HAD I...**

There was no way I was going to miss the opportunity to do this very same thing for my family!

My wife and I do not have any children of our own, so we made the decision to do this very same thing for our nieces and nephews.

As of the date of publication, my 26-year-old nephew is a respiratory therapist; my 22-year-old nephew is an electrician; my 12-year-old niece loves art and music; and my 6-year-old niece loves to sing, dance, run and play.

I am fairly certain that none of them will ever be interested in:

- Reading a business journal
- Crunching numbers on a spreadsheet
- Learning how inflation affects the economy
- Figuring out whether the Fed increasing the interest rate is good or not.

And quite frankly, I'm not interested in them <u>HAVING</u> to do that either.

And this is what led me to write this book.

The idea is for this book to be the only thing my nieces and nephews ever HAVE to read in order to understand exactly why they need to save and invest money for their retirement, exactly what to invest their money in, and why.

<u>In short, I am preparing them to eventually take over the retirement account that my wife and I have set up for each of them so they can retire wealthy.</u>

Even more importantly, I want my nephews and nieces to understand exactly WHY they need to set up a ROTH IRA for their children and their children's children... **the moment they are born**... in order to continue creating **GENERATIONAL WEALTH** for our family... long after I am dead and gone.

And when the time comes for my nephews and nieces to start teaching their future children/grandchildren about investing... all they should have to do is give them this book to read.

This book started out as a 14-page instructional guide for my family. But the more I wrote, the more I realized how much of an impact this investment strategy could have on my friends' children and grandchildren. Then I began to think of my employees' children and grandchildren as well as THEIR friends and families' children and grandchildren.

That is when I made the decision to do my best to get this out to the masses.

I am very happy this book has ended up in your hands! Let's get started on building YOUR legacy and creating GENERATIONAL WEALTH for your family, too!

PLEASE NOTE

This book is simply my opinion. I am not a financial advisor, CPA, tax expert or fortune teller. I am simply an uncle who wants to share some of the lessons, insights and thought processes that I have gained over the span of a lifetime. The average annual growth rates I use in this book are not predictions of any sort; they are only being used for educational purposes.

And I want to be crystal clear about something:

The investment strategy I discuss in this book is nothing new and it isn't Earth-shattering:

- ROTH IRA's have been around for decades

- Setting up a ROTH IRA for a newborn baby was something I learned from my friend and mentor (Cecil)

- **Warren Buffett, the most prolific investor of all time**, has said on multiple occasions that all the average investors need to do is invest in nothing but the S&P 500 Index for decades and they will outperform 90% of the people in the market... including professional money managers.

This investment strategy is safe and simple. In fact, the hardest part of this entire strategy is it can be boring. There is NOTHING sexy or exciting about it. In my opinion, the S&P 500 is the safest bet on the planet and there is no reason to do anything but buy as many shares as you possibly can... as often as you can... and hold those shares until the day you die... Nothing more... Nothing less. This entire book has been written to explain exactly how you should do this...and why.

This investment strategy is the proverbial tortoise in the race against the hare.

<u>Remember, the tortoise wins the race... every time.</u>

And when it comes to **CREATING GENERATIONAL WEALTH**, winning is the only thing that matters!

The goal of this book is to show you exactly how to create **GENERATIONAL WEALTH** for yourself, your children and grandchildren with:

- No need for opinions from talking heads on television
- No need to have a business or finance degree (although having one is awesome!)
- No need to have a college degree
- No need to worry about the stock market going up
- No need to worry about the stock market going down
- No need to worry about the stock market going sideways
- No need to make a bunch of trades over the years wasting your time, energy and money

...And to create your family's **GENERATIONAL WEALTH** confidently!

This book has been written with these things in mind:

- If you are a parent or grandparent: I want you to be able to read this book in just a few hours, be able to easily understand the concepts and walk away knowing exactly why you should do everything humanly possible to IMMEDIATELY set up a retirement account for your children and grandchildren. It will be a life-changing, Family Tree Altering Decision! By the way, the younger they are, the better! Newborns... Yahtzee!

- If you are a high school or college student: I want you to be able to read this book in just a few hours, be able to easily understand all of the concepts, and be able to explain it to your friends, family and teachers. And most importantly, I want you to be able to immediately start investing for yourself using the strategy outlined in this book.

- Regardless of your age or education, I want you, the reader, to walk away from this book KNOWING that investing for your retirement as well as your children's and grandchildren's retirement is vitally important... and the sooner you do it, the better. And I also want you to walk away from this book KNOWING that you will be able to EASILY do this YOURSELF... and do it just as well or better than some professional that you would have to pay to invest your money for you.

This book is a simple read. The concepts are very easy to follow and the math is nothing more than simple addition, subtraction and multiplication. Anyone with a 10th grade education should be able to read this book and understand it.

All it will take is a few hours of your time. But I can assure you, the return on your time invested will be lifechanging for you, your children and your children's children!

You can go to **www.ButchMauldin.com** for more information. You can also reach me via email: **info@ButchMauldin.com** or on Facebook.

Thank you again for taking the time to read this. I wish you all the best! And please remember that I am rooting for you!

Chapter 1

EXACTLY HOW DOES $1,000 GROW INTO $256,000?

Let's take $1,000 and double it 8 times:

1st Time	$2,000.00
2nd Time	$4,000.00
3rd Time	$8,000.00
4th Time	$16,000.00
5th Time	$32,000.00
6th Time	$64,000.00
7th Time	$128,000.00
8th Time	$256,000.00

Think about what this means…If you can take $1,000 and have it double itself 8 times, that $1,000 will **magically** turn into $256,000… Don't believe me?

Let's take a hypothetical trip to the casino so I can prove these numbers are real. Let's walk straight up to the roulette table, place $1,000 on red and spin that wheel… If it lands on red, we've just doubled our $1,000 investment and we now have $2,000.

Now, let's do it again! Let's bet the entire $2,000 on red …and if we get lucky and it hits red, our money will double itself for a 2nd time, and we now have $4,000!

If we can get lucky enough to win 6 more times, our money will grow (compound) into $256,000… in less than 20 minutes!

DON'T DO THIS! GAMBLING IS NOT AN INVESTMENT STRATEGY. THIS IS JUST A WAY FOR ME TO CLARIFY THE CONCEPT OF COMPOUND GROWTH FOR YOU.

Gambling is obviously not a sound investment strategy. The likelihood of winning 8 times in a row is less than 1%, which means you will have over a 99% chance of losing your entire investment. **And losing your investment is NOT an option!**

As you will see… turning $1,000 into $256,000 is possible…. It's just going to take a lot longer than 20 minutes to do it.

The best way to have your $1,000 double itself is to invest it into something **very safe** that you can expect to grow consistently over several decades…

If you recall, **Warren Buffet, the most prolific investor of all time,** has said on multiple occasions that all the average American needs to do is invest in nothing but the S&P 500 Index and he/she will outperform 90% of the people in the market…including professional money managers. *[Don't worry, I will explain exactly what the S&P 500 is and why it is the safest bet on the planet in Chapter 2].*

SO, HOW LONG CAN WE EXPECT IT TO TAKE FOR LITTLE LUCIE'S $1,000 TO DOUBLE IN VALUE IF IT IS INVESTED IN THE S&P 500? AND HOW MUCH CAN WE EXPECT IT TO GROW TO IN THE NEXT 64 YEARS?

The S&P 500 has had an average annual growth rate of **approximately 9%*** for the past 30 years (1991-2021). For this exercise, we are going to assume the S&P 500 will continue to grow at this pace for the next 70 years:

Using these assumptions, we can use what is known as the Rule of 72 to determine how often we can expect the S&P 500 to double in value.**

The Rule of 72: 72 / 9 = 8 Years

This very simple calculation tells us that we can expect the S&P 500 to double in value every 8 years. This is just like the roulette table.

The only differences are:

- It takes 8 years for each game to play out
- There is a 99% chance you will win!

Although the S&P 500 realized this growth rate from 1991-2021, it does not mean it will continue to do so. This is just an example for educational purposes.

**Rule of 72 as defined by Caroline Banton (www.investopedia.com)*

Table 3: Rule of 72: 72 / 9 = 8 Years to Double

RULE OF 72 EXAMPLE:		
Expected Annual Growth Rate:		9.00%
Investment Amount:		$1,000
Expect to Double Every ___ Years		8.00
Rule of 72 = (72 / 9)		
	Year	Expected Value of Investment
	8	$2,000.00
	16	$4,000.00
	24	$8,000.00
	32	$16,000.00
	40	$32,000.00
	48	$64,000.00
	56	$128,000.00
	64	$256,000.00

By using this simple calculation, we can easily determine that $1,000 invested in the S&P 500 should compound into approximately $256,000 in approximately 64 years (assuming it continues growing at an annual rate of 9%).

I DON'T WANT YOU TO SIMPLY BELIEVE THESE NUMBERS
MAKE ME PROVE THEM TO YOU

So far, all I have done is throw a bunch of numbers at you. I need to take some time to show you exactly how the math works so you can trust these numbers. **Once YOU know these numbers are real, I am certain nothing will stop you from making this happen!**

I will tell you now that this section might be a little boring for you (*especially if you don't like math*), but you do need to learn and understand it… that is the bad news. The good news is, you don't have to memorize this math. All you need to do is learn enough of the math to understand exactly how compound growth works and why you can have full faith and trust in the numbers that you see in Table 3 (which was calculated based on the Rule of 72).

The process I am about to walk you through is what changed my life forever!

The first time I created a table like this was when I was taking a finance class in college. I was studying for a test. I was getting the correct answers, but I was frustrated because I simply didn't understand why or how these numbers were coming up on my calculator. **My lack of understanding caused me not to trust what I was seeing, so I made the decision to build a table like this on a spreadsheet… and that is when I was finally able to see exactly how and why these numbers added up.**

That was the single most important exercise I have ever performed when it came to understanding compound growth. At that moment, I knew without question that these numbers were real… that I could trust them 100%… and that was the moment I decided to start putting the magic of compound growth to work for me!

I would now like to walk you through exactly what I saw that day:

Table 4

\$1,000 Invested For 65 Years 9% Growth Rate		
Year	**Beginning Value**	**Growth For the Year**	**Ending Value**
1	\$1,000.00	\$90.00	\$1,090.00
2	\$1,090.00	\$98.10	\$1,188.10
3	\$1,188.10	\$106.93	\$1,295.03
4	\$1,295.03	\$116.55	\$1,411.58
5	\$1,411.58	\$127.04	\$1,538.62
6	\$1,538.62	\$138.48	\$1,677.10
7	\$1,677.10	\$150.94	\$1,828.04
8	\$1,828.04	\$164.52	\$1,992.56
9	\$1,992.56	\$179.33	\$2,171.89
10	\$2,171.89	\$195.47	\$2,367.36
11	\$2,367.36	\$213.06	\$2,580.43
12	\$2,580.43	\$232.24	\$2,812.66
13	\$2,812.66	\$253.14	\$3,065.80
14	\$3,065.80	\$275.92	\$3,341.73
15	\$3,341.73	\$300.76	\$3,642.48
16	\$3,642.48	\$327.82	\$3,970.31
17	\$3,970.31	\$357.33	\$4,327.63
18	\$4,327.63	\$389.49	\$4,717.12
19	\$4,717.12	\$424.54	\$5,141.66
20	\$5,141.66	\$462.75	\$5,604.41
21	\$5,604.41	\$504.40	\$6,108.81
22	\$6,108.81	\$549.79	\$6,658.60
23	\$6,658.60	\$599.27	\$7,257.87
24	\$7,257.87	\$653.21	\$7,911.08

Please take a moment to look at each line in Table 4 to verify my math.

In the first year, the $1,000 investment will be expected to grow by $90.00 ($1,000 x 9%) giving it an ending value of $1,090.00 after year one.

In year two, it will be expected to grow by another $98.10 ($1,090 x 9%) leaving it worth $1,188.10 after year 2. As you follow Table 4 down, year by year, until you get to the end of year 8, you will see that the original $1,000 investment is expected to grow to be valued at $1,992.56… nearly double the initial investment!

Look how closely the rule of 72 allows you to figure this out without having to build a table like this!

Now, look at the end of year 16… the investment is expected to double again from $1,992.56 to $3,970.31… and then it is expected to double again to $7,911.08 at the end of year 24.

Again, look how the rule of 72 allows you to figure this out in your head… without a calculator or spreadsheet!

TABLE 4 (Continued)

25	$7,911.08	$712.00	$8,623.08
26	$8,623.08	$776.08	$9,399.16
27	$9,399.16	$845.92	$10,245.08
28	$10,245.08	$922.06	$11,167.14
29	$11,167.14	$1,005.04	$12,172.18
30	$12,172.18	$1,095.50	$13,267.68
31	$13,267.68	$1,194.09	$14,461.77
32	$14,461.77	$1,301.56	$15,763.33
33	$15,763.33	$1,418.70	$17,182.03
34	$17,182.03	$1,546.38	$18,728.41
35	$18,728.41	$1,685.56	$20,413.97
36	$20,413.97	$1,837.26	$22,251.23
37	$22,251.23	$2,002.61	$24,253.84
38	$24,253.84	$2,182.85	$26,436.68
39	$26,436.68	$2,379.30	$28,815.98
40	$28,815.98	$2,593.44	$31,409.42
41	$31,409.42	$2,826.85	$34,236.27
42	$34,236.27	$3,081.26	$37,317.53
43	$37,317.53	$3,358.58	$40,676.11
44	$40,676.11	$3,660.85	$44,336.96
45	$44,336.96	$3,990.33	$48,327.29
46	$48,327.29	$4,349.46	$52,676.74
47	$52,676.74	$4,740.91	$57,417.65
48	$57,417.65	$5,167.59	$62,585.24
49	$62,585.24	$5,632.67	$68,217.91
50	$68,217.91	$6,139.61	$74,357.52
51	$74,357.52	$6,692.18	$81,049.70
52	$81,049.70	$7,294.47	$88,344.17
53	$88,344.17	$7,950.98	$96,295.14
54	$96,295.14	$8,666.56	$104,961.71
55	$104,961.71	$9,446.55	$114,408.26
56	$114,408.26	$10,296.74	$124,705.01
57	$124,705.01	$11,223.45	$135,928.46
58	$135,928.46	$12,233.56	$148,162.02
59	$148,162.02	$13,334.58	$161,496.60
60	$161,496.60	$14,534.69	$176,031.29
61	$176,031.29	$15,842.82	$191,874.11
62	$191,874.11	$17,268.67	$209,142.78
63	$209,142.78	$18,822.85	$227,965.63
64	$227,965.63	$20,516.91	$248,482.53
65	$248,482.53	$22,363.43	$270,845.96

As you follow this table down, year after year, you will see the POWER of compounding your money. What starts off as a small amount in year 1 slowly builds size and momentum just like a snowball rolling down a mountain. And then it turns into a monster... $248,482.53... and the really amazing thing is that you can expect that monster to pay you $22,363.43 every year for the rest of your life!

Again... This Is Only $1,000 Invested!

Now, let's take a look at the table I used to calculate my assumptions for Little Lucie in Chapter 1: $1,000 per year invested for 65 years with an average growth rate of 9%:

Table 5:

$1,000 Per Year Invested For 65 Years 9% Growth Rate			
Year	Beginning Value	Growth For The Year	Ending Value
1	$1,000.00	$90.00	$1,090.00
2	$2,090.00	$188.10	$2,278.10
3	$3,278.10	$295.03	$3,573.13
4	$4,573.13	$411.58	$4,984.71
5	$5,984.71	$538.62	$6,523.33
6	$7,523.33	$677.10	$8,200.43
7	$9,200.43	$828.04	$10,028.47
8	$11,028.47	$992.56	$12,021.04
9	$13,021.04	$1,171.89	$14,192.93
10	$15,192.93	$1,367.36	$16,560.29
11	$17,560.29	$1,580.43	$19,140.72
12	$20,140.72	$1,812.66	$21,953.38
13	$22,953.38	$2,065.80	$25,019.19
14	$26,019.19	$2,341.73	$28,360.92
15	$29,360.92	$2,642.48	$32,003.40
16	$33,003.40	$2,970.31	$35,973.70
17	$36,973.70	$3,327.63	$40,301.34
18	$41,301.34	$3,717.12	$45,018.46
19	$46,018.46	$4,141.66	$50,160.12
20	$51,160.12	$4,604.41	$55,764.53
21	$56,764.53	$5,108.81	$61,873.34
22	$62,873.34	$5,658.60	$68,531.94
23	$69,531.94	$6,257.87	$75,789.81
24	$76,789.81	$6,911.08	$83,700.90
25	$84,700.90	$7,623.08	$92,323.98
26	$93,323.98	$8,399.16	$101,723.13
27	$102,723.13	$9,245.08	$111,968.22
28	$112,968.22	$10,167.14	$123,135.36
29	$124,135.36	$11,172.18	$135,307.54
30	$136,307.54	$12,267.68	$148,575.22
31	$149,575.22	$13,461.77	$163,036.99
32	$164,036.99	$14,763.33	$178,800.32
33	$179,800.32	$16,182.03	$195,982.34
34	$196,982.34	$17,728.41	$214,710.75

Table 5 (Continued):

35	$215,710.75	$19,413.97	$235,124.72
36	$236,124.72	$21,251.23	$257,375.95
37	$258,375.95	$23,253.84	$281,629.78
38	$282,629.78	$25,436.68	$308,066.46
39	$309,066.46	$27,815.98	$336,882.45
40	$337,882.45	$30,409.42	$368,291.87
41	$369,291.87	$33,236.27	$402,528.13
42	$403,528.13	$36,317.53	$439,845.66
43	$440,845.66	$39,676.11	$480,521.77
44	$481,521.77	$43,336.96	$524,858.73
45	$525,858.73	$47,327.29	$573,186.02
46	$574,186.02	$51,676.74	$625,862.76
47	$626,862.76	$56,417.65	$683,280.41
48	$684,280.41	$61,585.24	$745,865.65
49	$746,865.65	$67,217.91	$814,083.56
50	$815,083.56	$73,357.52	$888,441.08
51	$889,441.08	$80,049.70	$969,490.77
52	$970,490.77	$87,344.17	$1,057,834.94
53	$1,058,834.94	$95,295.14	$1,154,130.09
54	$1,155,130.09	$103,961.71	$1,259,091.80
55	$1,260,091.80	$113,408.26	$1,373,500.06
56	$1,374,500.06	$123,705.01	$1,498,205.06
57	$1,499,205.06	$134,928.46	$1,634,133.52
58	$1,635,133.52	$147,162.02	$1,782,295.53
59	$1,783,295.53	$160,496.60	$1,943,792.13
60	$1,944,792.13	$175,031.29	$2,119,823.42
61	$2,120,823.42	$190,874.11	$2,311,697.53
62	$2,312,697.53	$208,142.78	$2,520,840.31
63	$2,521,840.31	$226,965.63	$2,748,805.94
64	$2,749,805.94	$247,482.53	$2,997,288.47
65	$2,998,288.47	$269,845.96	$3,268,134.44

Just take a look at those numbers. Do the calculations manually on a calculator for the first 10 years and get to where you KNOW these numbers are real. If you do this, nothing will stop you from creating **YOUR LEGACY** and creating **GENERATIONAL WEALTH** for yourself, your children and your children's children!

Stop for a minute and really think about what you are seeing here: $1,000 per year compounded at 9% can be expected to morph into nearly $3 MILLION in 65 years! And this beautiful monster can then be expected to feed your child/grandchild nearly **$270,000 PER YEAR!**

...Year After Year...

For the rest of his/her life...TAX FREE!

And then this beautiful $2.6 million monster can then be passed on to the next generation!

What a legacy!

NOW DO YOU SEE WHY LITTLE LUCIE HIT THE JACKPOT?!

Now, let's talk about the exponential power of time and why I want you to set up a retirement account for your child/grandchild as soon as humanly possible!

Example 1:

Let's say I am 25 years old and looking to invest $2,000 into the S&P 500, and I expect the average annual growth rate of this investment to be 9%... How much can I expect my $2,000 investment to compound into 40 years from now?

Let's use the Rule of 72 to determine how often I can expect this investment to double in value:

72 / 9 = 8

So, I am expecting this investment to double itself every 8 years.

I expect to hold this investment for 40 years, so this investment should double itself 5 times...

That is because **40 / 8 = 5**

So, this is what I can expect my $2,000 to grow to over the next 40 years:

Year	Value of Investment
0	$2,000
8	$4,000
16	$8,000
24	$16,000
32	$32,000
40	$40,000

**My investment is expected to double in value 5 times

Example 2:

Let's say you are investing $1,000 into the S&P 500 for your two-year-old grandchild and you expect the average annual growth rate of this investment to be 8%... How much can you expect your $1,000 investment to compound to 65 years from now?

Let's use the Rule of 72 to determine how often you can expect this investment to double in value:

72 / 8 = 9

So, YOU are expecting this investment to double itself every 9 years *(that is 1 year longer than what I am expecting for my investment)*

And you are expecting your grandchild to hold this investment for 63 years, so this investment should double itself 7 times...

That is because **63 / 9 = 7**

So, this is what you can expect your $1,000 to grow to over the next 65 years:

Year	Value of Investment
0	$1,000
9	$2,000
18	$4,000
27	$8,000
36	$16,000
45	$32,000
54	$64,000
63	$128,000

**Your grandchild's investment is expected to double in value 7 times

Now let's take a closer look at your investment for your grandchild vs mine and let's see what we can learn:

Table 6:

	MY INVESTMENT	YOUR GRANDCHILD'S INVESTMENT
Initial Investment	$2,000.00	$1,000.00
Years to Invest	40	63
Expected Avg. Annual Growth	9%	8%
Expected Value at End of Investment	$64,000.00	$128,000.00

- **You are investing half the money I am**
- **You are expecting a smaller percentage of growth**
- **But you are expecting your grandchild's investment to be worth double ($128,000 vs $64,000) what I expect mine to be worth...**

HOW IS THAT POSSIBLE?

THE ANSWER IS TIME!

The extra 20 years that your grandchild's investment has to use the power of compound growth is the difference. That extra 20 years will allow your $1,000 investment to double in value 7 times versus only 5 times for mine! **This is why it is so important to start saving and investing for yourself, your children and/or your grandchildren as soon as humanly possible!**

Please Do Not Read Any Further Until You Trust These Numbers… Until You Know They Are Real… And You Understand Exactly What They Are Telling You!

Chapter 2

THE SAFEST BET ON THE PLANET!

The S&P 500!

There is nothing safer than investing your money into the top 500 publicly traded companies in the United States of America... period.

Not only is this the safest bet on the planet, but you will be hard pressed to find another investment that will provide you with a higher expected average annual growth rate over a long period of time! When I say a long period of time, I am talking about 55-65 years (for your children and grandchildren).

By the way, these 500 publicly traded companies are known as the S&P 500.

And luckily, you and I can invest in all 500 of these companies by simply purchasing shares of an "Exchange Traded Fund" (ETF) known as a Spyder (SPDR). **The trading symbol is SPY** That's right... all you have to do is buy one share of a **SPY** and your money is magically invested in the top 500 publicly traded companies in America!

So, what are Spyders (SPDRs) and what do they have to do with the S&P 500?

- ✓ A SPDR is what is known as an "Exchange Traded Fund (ETF)"
- ✓ The reason for an ETF's existence is to mirror a specific Index
- ✓ The SPDR is the ETF that mirrors the S&P 500
- ✓ You can purchase SPDRs through any online brokerage account – **its symbol is SPY**
- ✓ One share of SPY is equal to approximately 1/10 of the S&P 500
- ✓ When you purchase a share of SPY, you are in essence purchasing 1/10 of a share of each of the 500 companies that make up the S&P 500 (Max Diversification!)
- ✓ If the S&P 500 drops by 2%, you can expect your shares of SPY to mirror that decline in value
- ✓ If the S&P 500 increases by 7%, you can expect your shares of SPY to mirror that increase

The brilliance of "Exchange Traded Funds" (ETFs) like SPY is they allow investors like you and me to literally purchase all of the stocks that make up a specific Index and only have to make one trade in order to make it happen! This saves you and me a lot of time, a lot of money and a lot of hassle.

By the way, you can purchase ETFs for Indexes in most all of the Stock Exchanges throughout the world. And there are several American ETFs that you can choose from as well. But I have chosen to invest mine and my family's money in only one ETF… SPY. **And that is because it mirrors the S&P 500.**

Please allow me to provide you with the reasons I believe there is no safer bet on the planet than the S&P 500:

REASON #1

In the 20th century (1900-1999), the U.S. economy grew by more than tenfold. Now stop and think about this for a moment. During this 100-year span, the U.S. economy had some pretty major disasters to deal with:

- The Spanish Flu killed millions of Americans
- World War I
- The Great Depression
- World War II
- The Korean War
- Vietnam
- The Cold War
- The Gas Shortages of the 1970s
- The Iran Hostage Situation
- The Cuban Missile Crisis
- The Assassination of two presidents
- Hurricanes, Tornadoes and Many Other Natural Disasters

The list of difficulties and hardships during this century goes on and on and on.

But even with all of these setbacks and all the bad news that we see every single day of our lives... The U.S. economy soared to new heights and became the biggest, strongest, most powerful economy this world has ever seen.

The combination of America's:

- Abundant resources

- Rich history

- Diversity

- Constitution and Bill of Rights

- Legal system

- Capitalism

Has created a very strong foundation for the U.S. economy.

REASON #2

Now let's think about exactly who is truly vested in the American economy prospering...

You
Me
Your Family
Teachers
Fire Fighters
Police Officers
Small Business Owners
Medium-Sized Business Owners
CEOs of Large Corporations
Executives In All Sized Businesses
Middle Managers
...and everyone in between

Anyone who has a job or wants a job has a vested interest in the American economy prospering.

But that's not all... Who else has a vested interest in the American economy prospering?

Financial Advisors
People with money invested in the stock market
Parents who dream of a better life for their children

All of whom are...

VOTERS

And that brings us to the profound part of this question I've asked you to really stop and consider:

Who has a vested interest in the American economy prospering?

Your Mayor
Your City Councilmen
Your State Senators
Your State Congressmen
Your U.S. Congressmen
Your U.S. Senators
Your Federal Judges
Your Supreme Court Justices
The U.S. Treasury Department

THE PRESIDENT OF THE UNITED STATES

Think about it. Every single one of these people have a vested interest in the U.S. economy prospering. But that isn't the biggest part... here it is...

Every single one of these people will do anything – I mean whatever it takes – to keep the American economy from ever failing, because if that were to ever happen, we would all be living in a Great Depression... and trust me... no one wants that... especially our elected leaders.

Without a strong, prospering economy, they don't get re-elected. And if they don't get re-elected, they are out of power... and that is the worst thing that can happen to a politician.

Never forget this and you will never be afraid of bad news again!

THE U.S. ECONOMY HAS THE FULL WEIGHT AND FORCE OF THE PRESIDENT OF THE UNITED STATES OF AMERICA, EVERY PERSON WHO WORKS FOR HIM, EVERY ELECTED OFFICIAL FROM YOUR LOCAL COMMUNITY ALL THE WAY TO WASHINGTON... HELL BENT ON MAKING IT PROSPER

Just look at what happened in 2007. The U.S. Treasurer literally came out and told the country we were in the beginning stages of the American housing industry collapsing on itself.

Just take a look at what the President of the United States and every elected official did to save the economy. **They printed money and gave it away like it was going out of style. They literally gave billions away to large corporations to save them from bankruptcy and they saved millions upon millions of jobs in the process.** In short, they stopped us from entering into a Great Depression... they literally saved every American from losing their retirement savings!

After that, they rushed to enact new rules and guidelines to shore up the problem and to make sure it never happened again. In the end... they saved the economy... we all did!

Then take a look at what the President of the United States and every elected official did in 2020 when COVID came into existence. **Again, they printed money like it was going out of style and this time, they gave that money away to everyone... citizens, business owners, cities, states... everyone. Without them doing this, the economy would have collapsed into oblivion. We would all be living in the 1800s right now as we speak. Our elected officials knew this... and because they had a vested interest in saving this economy, they did what it took.**

I can't tell you what challenges our economy will face over the next 10, 20, 30, or 40 years... but I can tell you this... whatever comes our way... **the U.S. economy... and these 500 publicly traded companies that make up the S&P 500 will always have the full weight and force of the American people, the President of the United States, everyone who works for him, as well as every elected official... local, state and federal.**

So, when bad new hits, just relax and let all of these smart, powerful people go to work for you!

REASON #3

Over the past 30 years, the S&P 500 has had an average annual growth rate of 8.59%.

During that time, this country went through:

> ➢ The Gulf War
> ➢ Two Presidential Impeachment Trials
> ➢ 9/11
> ➢ The Bombing of the World Trade Center
> ➢ Afghan War
> ➢ The Housing Bubble Crisis of 2007
> ➢ Mad Cow Disease Scare
> ➢ COVID
> ➢ Hurricane Katrina

All of these awful, scary things happened... yet the market kept moving up at an average of 8.59% per year. By the way, this is why I chose to use 9% in the examples in previous chapters.

Think about this for a moment: Had I set up a ROTH IRA for my oldest nephew when he was born in 1995 and purchased $1,000 **per year** in **SPY** for him, his ROTH IRA would now be worth over $91,000 just 26 years later!

I am so disappointed that I didn't know to do this for him back then! What a missed opportunity! Don't allow yourself to miss this opportunity for your children and grandchildren!

BUT... HINDSIGHT IS ALWAYS 20/20, SO LET'S LEARN FROM THE PAST SO WE CAN CAPITALIZE ON THE FUTURE

Now, just imagine having read this book in 1991 and being too scared to buy into the market when the news was bad... Just imagine how you would feel 30 years later knowing that had you just followed the investment strategy in this book, how much better off you would be in retirement. Even with all of the bad things that happened from 1991-2021...the market still grew... why?

Look, there are always going to be bad things that happen in our country. Scary things that will keep us up at night worrying about our future and our children's futures. There will be wars, and there will be bad days, weeks, months... even bad years that our economy will have to face over the next 20, 30, 40, 50 plus years *(as you will see in the next chapter)*. But know this... no matter what... smart people will be getting up every single day and doing everything in their power to ensure this country stays intact **and this economy keeps prospering.**

And no matter what... parents will wake up every single day... **no matter how hard it is**... to put food on the table and to figure out exactly how they can do their part to make it where their children have even better opportunities than they have had.

So don't worry about the bad news... it's coming... but know this: The American economy is built not only to endure the bad times... but to prosper in them!

Something else we can learn from the past 30 years is no one... and I do mean no one... can predict the market. So, don't worry about trying to figure out the best time to invest your money... **just make it an automatic process and live your life. Don't fret over it... that is a total waste of time.**

All you need to do is pay your "FUTURE" self as much money as you possibly can, deposit it into your ROTH IRA and put all of those smart, rich, powerful people to work for you... then all you need to do is to just relax and go live your life!

In other words, save as much money as possible and invest it ALL into the U.S. economy by purchasing as many SPDRs as you possibly can... as often as you can!

REASON #4

Here are a few more things I would like you to consider about these 500 companies known as the S&P 500:

The S&P 500 is what investors call "The Market." It is an Index of how the market is performing. Basically, it is the Index for the U.S. Economy. These 500 companies are selected by a committee of financial experts who research all of the publicly traded companies in America. In short, only the best publicly traded companies get into and stay in the S&P 500.

Each of these 500 companies have:

> - The smartest, most highly compensated executives running them
> - Boat loads of cash to use for Research and Development
> - Deep ties to local, state and federal politicians
> - Purchasing power
> - Best name recognition in their prospective industries
> - Highly compensated lobbyists
> - Most up-to-date technological advances at their disposal
> - And much more!

My point is this: The S&P 500 is made up of the best known, most successful businesses in America. **And these 500 companies have the full weight and force of the U.S. President, his staff, every politician across this great land of ours and every voter, too.**

There is no safer bet than these 500 companies… Period.

Take a moment to really think about what I am about to say here:

If the most prolific investor of all time says that you are going to do better than 90% of investors by simply investing in the S&P 500

AND

If you believe that investing your money in the top 500 publicly traded companies in the Unites States is the safest bet on the planet

...Then why would you choose to do anything else, but this?!

Hopefully, you now see why I believe that investing all of your retirement savings into the S&P 500 is the safest bet on the planet!

 There is no other way I can think of to be more diversified than by investing in the U.S. Economy (S&P 500)

 No other investment that I can think of has the full weight and force of the Federal Government

 Very few investors were able to average more than 8.59% in average annual growth over the past 30 years.

 I can't think of any money managers that I am certain can beat the S&P 500 over the next 30 years

 I can't think of any other investment that will allow me to go on with my life and not HAVE to study business journals or listen to talking heads on TV

 Warren Buffet, the most prolific investor in history, says this is the best way for the average American to invest

Simply put, by choosing to invest all of my retirement into the S&P 500, I feel confident that I am maximizing my returns while minimizing my risk...

How About You?

Chapter 3

WHO CARES IF THE MARKET DROPS 5 YEARS IN A ROW?

Ok, let's pretend that you read this book back in 2000 and decided you were going to set up a ROTH IRA and fund it with enough money to buy 7 shares of SPY:

	High on June 1	Value of 7 Shares
2000	$149.16	$1,044.12

And let's say that you were the person who bought it at highest price of the entire day! **Unlucky you!**

You are so excited because the market has been growing like a weed, the media is talking about the huge expected growth of the economy over the next few years, and you've just read this awesome book that told you to put everything into the S&P 500 and just go live your life!

And you are thinking to yourself: 'Wow! I have all of these smart CEOs out there making me money and I have the President of the United States and every other elected official across this great country working hard to make sure this economy keeps booming!'

You know you shouldn't watch the price of your shares... but you just can't help yourself. At no point for the rest of the year does the price go above what you paid for it. You tell yourself, "Okay, it's only been 6 months, it's not a big deal. It doesn't matter what the price is today, it only matters what the price is in 40 years when I retire..."

You tell yourself this, but you certainly aren't as excited or as confident as you were when you bought these stinking shares! You know you need to just live your life. That's what that guy in that book you read kept saying. But you can't help yourself.

You tell yourself, "Surely the price will be higher a year after I bought these shares!"

	High on June 1	Value of 7 Shares
2001	$129.23	$904.61

But it isn't... they go lower!

You can't believe it! That $1,044.12 that you spent on these stupid shares are only worth $904.61! You are not happy and you tell yourself, "I lost $139.51 this past year!"

You get that old book out that you read last year, flip to Chapter 2, you re-read "THE SAFEST BET ON THE PLANET" and it helps you gain some more confidence.

Then you tell yourself, "It's okay. Next year will be better."

THEN THE UNTHINKABLE HAPPENS!

You wake up one Tuesday morning to a bright, sunny, cloudless day. The weather is perfect! This is going to be a great day! But... you are dead wrong...

Because today is Tuesday, September 11, 2001, and in an hour or so the World Trade Center towers will be no more. At that very moment, the entire world is turned upside down and it will never be the same.

Fear is rampant. Doom and gloom prevail.

The stock market takes a dive and it doesn't recover for the next 5 years!

	High on June 1	Value of 7 Shares
2001	$129.23	$904.61
2002	$107.60	$753.20
2003	$102.18	$715.26
2004	$114.94	$804.58
2005	$121.94	$853.58
2006	$129.43	$906.01

You take a look at the price of SPY only to see that six years after buying these stupid shares, you are still down $138.11!

You tell yourself, "This is stupid! I could have bought something really nice with that money! I've lost nearly $150... I think I am going to send a nasty email to the guy that wrote that book!"

You consider just selling the shares and cashing out, but you remember that you set this up as a retirement account and you can't. Now you are really unhappy with that author... "Where does that guy live?!"

Another year goes by and the market slumbers along. You simply can't believe your bad luck.

June 2007 rolls around and for the first time in the 7 years that you have owned these shares, they are actually worth more than you paid for them!

	High on June 1	Value of 7 Shares
2007	$154.40	$1,080.80

After 7 years, you are up a mind-numbing $36.68! So… your money has made you enough money to pay for one dinner. Some quick math tells you that your shares now have an average growth rate of 0.50% over the past 7 years. You tell yourself, "I am going to wring that author's neck!"

But you decide to be positive. The news has been good. Everyone is saying the market is going to boom this year… so you look to the future just knowing your shares are only going up from here!

WRONG AGAIN!

Bad news hits the airwaves! Secretary of Treasury, Hank Paulson, comes onto the television and tells the world that America has a housing bubble, combined with a national credit crisis… the world is stunned! Is America going broke? The market is shaken to its core for the next 2 years:

	High on June 1	Value of 7 Shares
2008	$140.89	$986.23
2009	$96.11	$672.77

You think to yourself, '9 years from the day I bought these stupid shares and I have lost $371.35!'

But you hang in there… You tell yourself:

- All 500 CEOs of the companies that make up the S&P 500 are doing everything they can to turn it around… as well as their employees.
- The U.S. economy has the full weight and force of the President of the United States as well as every other elected official across this great country doing everything possible to get things back on track.
- SPY is the safest bet on the planet.

So, you stay patient….

	High on June 1	Value of 7 Shares
2010	$113.20	$792.40
2011	$134.92	$944.44
2012	$136.27	$953.89
2013	$165.99	$1,161.93

It takes 4 more years before your shares are finally worth more than you paid for them 13 years ago! From 2000-2013, your money has only made you $117.81. You are not happy!

That author in that stupid book said I could expect my money to double itself every 8 years! Where did he get off with 9%?! I have only seen an average of 1%!

But you go back and re-read some chapters and decide to stay in it for the long haul. And it is a very good thing you did:

Because the next 8 years boom!

	High on June 1	Value of 7 Shares
2014	$196.60	$1,376.20
2015	$213.34	$1,493.38
2016	$212.52	$1,487.64
2017	$245.01	$1,715.07
2018	$279.48	$1,956.36
2019	$296.31	$2,074.17
2020	$323.41	$2,263.87
2021	$428.78	$3,001.46

From 2014-2021, your shares grow an average of 14.77% per year! And as of June 1, 2021, your shares are worth $3,001.46! Aren't you glad you bought these shares and held them?

Over the past 21 years, your shares have now had an average annual growth rate of 8.93%.

You think to yourself, 'Hmmm, maybe I need to send that author an apology email.'

"I really am glad I read his book! I am going to buy all of my friends and family members a copy right now!"

Here are some things we need to take away from this:

> You haven't lost anything when the price is low. The only way you would have lost is if you had actually sold your shares… which you didn't.

> No one has a clue as to what the average annual growth rate of the market will be next year, much less the next decade – especially not me! That's okay. Invest your money anyway. And I highly suggest you invest it into the "Safest Bet on the Planet" and let all of those smart, powerful people across this great country figure out the rest for you.

> It doesn't matter what the price is today. It matters what the price will be many decades from now when it is time for you to retire…

> This $1,000… had you not invested it… would have been spent on something that would most likely be out of your life and memory **two decades later**. In short, had you spent that $1,000, you certainly would have lost all of it… so don't fret over drops in the value of these shares.

> When you get nervous, go back and read this book again. The principles will not break.

> Buying shares one time is NOT a good investment strategy. You need to buy as many shares of SPY as often as you can in order to take advantage of the prices while they are cheap!

And always remember, the lower the price of SPY, the more shares you can purchase!

JUST LOOK AT HOW MANY SHARES $1,000 COULD BUY YOU IN 2009!

Table 6

	High on June 1	Shares Purchased
2000	$149.16	7
2001	$129.23	8
2002	$107.60	10
2003	$102.18	10
2004	$114.94	9
2005	$121.94	8
2006	$129.43	9
2007	$154.40	6
2008	$140.89	8
2009	$96.11	11
2010	$113.20	9
2011	$134.92	8
2012	$136.27	7
2013	$165.99	7
2014	$196.60	5
2015	$213.34	5
2016	$212.52	5
2017	$245.01	4
2018	$279.48	4
2019	$296.31	3
2020	$323.41	3
2021	$428.78	2
Shares of SPY:		148
Value of Shares:		$63,459.44

WHAT A BARGAIN!

IT'S ALL IN THE MINDSET

It is very easy to have that mindset when you are looking at historical prices. It isn't so easy when you are in the moment and everyone you know thinks the sky is falling. And it certainly doesn't help make it any easier when you have the news media and politicians telling us all how the world is going to fall apart if we don't do things their way. Just know this... it is all noise... tune it out.

Just take a look at this chart. $1,000 would only buy you two shares of SPY in June 2021. Compare that to 2009 when $1,000 would have allowed you to purchase 11 shares! Look at that bargain basement price!

That is the mindset I want you to have when you see the price of SPY dropping! Tell yourself, "I am never going to be able to buy it this cheap again!" ...Even if that ends up not being the case.

This is why Warren Buffet, the greatest investor in history, has said on multiple occasions that the best play for the average American is to systematically purchase shares of an ETF (like SPY) and hold them forever!

By the way, take another look at Table 6… This is what my 22-year-old nephew's ROTH IRA would look like today had I known about this concept when he was born. By simply investing $1,000 per year and buying as many shares of SPY as I could, my nephew's retirement account would have **148 shares of SPY valued at $63,459.44**. That is nearly triple what I would have contributed – $22,000 – even though SPY failed to average more than a 1% annual growth rate until 2013!

The real money would have been made when the price of SPY was very low (2000-2013). Interestingly enough, this is when many investors were most afraid to buy them.

Don't fall into that trap! And if you ever feel like you are… go back and re-read Chapter 2, "THE SAFEST BET ON THE PLANET."

<u>Every single time I look at Table 6, I think of how I missed this opportunity for my 22-year-old nephew…</u>

<u>Don't miss it for your children and grandchildren!</u>

Things To Always Remember:

- ✓ Buy as many shares of SPY as often as you possibly can

- ✓ The price does not matter today... only the day you retire

- ✓ Have the mindset that you will never be able to buy it any cheaper than you are able to today

- ✓ Have faith in the American economy

- ✓ Live!

Chapter 4

429,810 REASONS TO SET UP A ROTH!

Now let's take a very close look at how Lucie can expect to be able to live on $429,810 more during her retirement years, just because her grandfather set her up with a ROTH IRA

If you recall, Lucie's grandfather set up a ROTH IRA with the plan to invest a minimum of $1,000 per year until she is mature enough to start contributing into her ROTH IRA herself until she is 65 years old. Let's just assume that $1,000 is invested in Lucie's account each and every year for 65 years and this account actually grows at an average annual rate of 7%... (less than expected)

Let's also assume that Lucie will live to be 90 years old (retired for 25 years)… What she can expect:

INVESTED THROUGH A ROTH IRA

➤ Annual Contribution:	$1,000.00
➤ Total Years to Contribute:	65 Years
➤ Total Contribution into Your ROTH IRA:	$65,000
➤ Total Taxes Paid at Time of Investment:	$13,000
➤ Average Annual Growth Rate:	7.00%
➤ Expected Value of Lucie's ROTH IRA at age 65:	$1,228,028.02
➤ Amount Lucie Can Expect to Withdraw Annually:	$85,961.96
➤ Expected Tax Rate at Retirement:	20%
➤ Amount Lucie Can Expect to Live on Annually:	$85,961.96
➤ How Many Years Lucie Expects To Live Past Retirement:	25 Years
➤ Total Amount Lucie Expects to Live on After Retirement:	$2,149,049.00
➤ Expected Value of Lucie's ROTH at age 90:	$1,228,028.02
➤ Total Taxes Paid After Retirement:	$0
➤ Effective Tax Rate:	0.38%

Simply because Lucie's grandfather chose to set up a ROTH IRA for her, she can expect to be able to withdraw $85,961.96 each and every year from the time she turns 65 until the day she dies... **And she will be able to live on 100% of the money she is able to withdraw ...BECAUSE SHE WILL HAVE TO PAY NO TAXES ON THAT MONEY**... and she will be able to do that until the day she dies.

This means she will be able to withdraw more than $2,100,000.00 ($85,961.96 x 25 years) and live on 100% of that money... and then she will be able to pass the $1,228,028.02 that will be left over to her loved ones when she passes away.

Now, let's take a look at what Lucie could have expected to live on each year had her grandfather NOT chosen to set her up with a ROTH IRA:

CHOOSING NOT TO INVEST THROUGH A ROTH IRA

- Annual Contribution: $1,000.00
- Total Years to Contribute: 65 Years
- Total Contribution into Your ROTH IRA: $65,000
- Total Taxes Paid at Time of Investment: $0
- Actual Average Annual Growth Rate: 7.00%
- Expected Value of Lucie's ROTH IRA at age 65: $1,228,028.02
- Amount Lucie Can Expect to Withdraw Annually: $85,961.96
- Expected Tax Rate at Retirement: 20%
- Amount Lucie Can Expect to Live on Annually: $68,769.57
- How Many Years Lucie Expects To Live Past Retirement: 25 Years
- Total Amount Lucie Expects to Live on After Retirement: $2,149,049.00
- Expected Value of Lucie's ROTH at age 90: $1,228,028.02
- Total Taxes Paid After Retirement: $429,810.00
- Effective Tax Rate: 9.60%

Based on this scenario, Lucie could still expect to withdraw $85,961.96 each and every year from the time she turns 65 until the day she dies... but she would have to pay taxes on that money, which means she would only be able to live on 80% of what she took out... which is only $68,769.57 per year.

This means she would still be able to withdraw over $2,100,000 ($85,961.96 x 25 years), but she could only live on $1,719,239.20 ($68,769.57 x 25 years), because the rest would all be paid in taxes... **that is a $429,810 difference!**

This is how Lucie's grandfather generated an estimated $429,810.00 more for her to live on after retirement by simply choosing to set her up with a ROTH IRA!

Chapter 5

TIME FOR SOME BRUTAL HONESTY

I would like to dedicate this chapter to my cousin's 18-year-old son, Waylon.

This Christmas, I drove over to see my cousin and her family. I have only had the opportunity to see them a handful of times over the past few years, so I made sure to take some time to go by and see them. We sat around talking about what was going on in each other's lives, cracked a few jokes at each other's expense (that's what my family loves to do… we are experts at it!) and most importantly, we took a little time to enjoy one another's company.

After an hour or so, I stood up to leave and was saying my goodbyes when my cousin's husband asked me to sit back down and tell Waylon a little about myself and my life's story.

I was taken aback by that notion, because up until that point, we were all joking around, laughing and having a good time.

And I was literally in the process of leaving.

Furthermore, I had never had any type of conversation with Waylon other than to ask him about his baseball games.

A quick side note: Waylon is a freshman in college and he is the first in our family to ever play baseball at the collegiate level… something we are all very proud of.

But I understood exactly what his dad was wanting me to do and why. So, I looked straight at Waylon and asked him if that was something he was interested in hearing. He said absolutely. He told me he wanted to own his own business someday and he wanted to be rich.

That was all I needed to hear. For the next 30 minutes, I told him my life's story and I answered all of the questions he had for me. He was very interested in how I ended up owning 13 rental houses that were paid for with cash. And he was very interested in how I was able to start a business from scratch and grow it to 11 locations in 4 states, with cash.

After answering all of his questions, I leaned in towards him, looked him straight in the eyes, paused for effect and then said this to him:

"If you only remember one thing I tell you tonight, make absolutely sure it is this. If you want to be wealthy, you do NOT have to own your own business. You do NOT have to be a major league baseball player and you do not have to make zillions of dollars per year. All you have to do is **SAVE** 15% of **EVERYTHING** you ever make in your life and invest it into a retirement account. Nothing more. Nothing less. That is, it. And when I say to save it, I mean never spend it... ever."

I could see it in his face. He did not like what I had just said to him.

I could only imagine the thoughts that were going through his mind.

Up until that moment, Waylon was focusing on the results I have been able to achieve so far in my 48 years on this Earth.

He was listening to my story and he was DREAMING about the day he would achieve them himself.

It was all fun and games until I said that to him.

That's when the next round of questions came. And let me tell you, they were serious questions. There was no dreaming going on anymore. That is because Waylon was now focusing on the dirty little details of what HE had to do if he really wanted to be rich.

The questions kept coming and the answers weren't what he wanted to hear.

Waylon looked straight at me and said, "I am not interested in doing that. If I make money, I want to have access to it and I want to be able to spend it whenever I want."

I didn't flinch. I looked right back at him and said, "Then you will never be wealthy. It is just a dream for you."

That really got his attention.

That is when I decided to use an analogy that would speak directly to him.

I said, "Waylon, let me ask you a question. Have you ever heard of anyone reaching the major leagues who refused to practice when they were in middle school, high school and college?"

He looked at me, laughed and said that he hadn't.

I explained to him that baseball players have to practice in order to build their skills and improve timing with their team mates. He nodded in agreement.

I then asked him this question, "Can you imagine a middle school kid asking you about how to become a collegiate baseball player and then him telling you that he absolutely refused to practice? What would you say to him?"

That's when he started to get the point. The scowling face went away and he was ready to hear me out.

I then began to explain that **<u>no one in the history of time has ever become wealthy and stayed wealthy unless they had a SAVER's mindset.</u>** Too many people in this country are consumers. If they make $1, they spend that entire $1... and then they will go borrow another $5 because they simply don't know how to turn off their "WANT BUTTON."

It was a moment of brutal honesty for Waylon. It was not a fun conversation, but it was something he had to hear, ponder on and then make his decision.

I can't wait for him to read this book so he will be able to have an even better understanding of the things we talked about that night (and I am sure he will think it's pretty cool that he has been mentioned in a book).

IT'S HARD TO GET RICH, IT'S HARD TO BE POOR... CHOOSE YOUR HARD

Saving and investing 15% of what you make is hard. It requires humility, patience and discipline. It requires you not to have every single thing you want... exactly when you want it... and it requires you to have less of the things that you could afford if you weren't saving and investing all of that money. **But this is a requirement if you really do want to become wealthy. There is no way around it. Pure and simple.**

Need some proof?

Please Google **"Celebrities who have gone bankrupt."**

Go look at all of the celebrities who have made tens of millions of dollars and went broke. These celebrities made a LOT of money... but they weren't wealthy. And when their bad spending habits caught up with them... they lost it all!

If you think being broke is bad. Try being rich... and then going broke.

I simply can't imagine!

Taking 15% of everything you ever make and investing for your future is hard. But so is living paycheck to paycheck and having to work until the day you die.

This is the point where you have to be brutally honest with yourself... and make a decision right now...

Which "Hard" do you choose?

Chapter 6

LET ME BLOW YOUR MIND!

$3,000,000 will be peanuts if Little Lucie does this one thing!

In chapter 1, I told you about the day my friend and mentor informed me that he had set up a ROTH IRA for his granddaughter, Little Lucie. If you recall, I went straight home with these two questions in mind… and these are the answers I calculated:

1. Assuming $1,000 per year is invested in Lucie's retirement account for the next 65 years and that account grows (compounds) at an average annual rate of 9%… how much will her retirement account be worth when she turns 65?

$2,998,288.47

2. How much can she expect to be able to live on each and every year after she reaches retirement age?

$269,845.96

What I didn't tell you at the time, is this is the bare minimum that Little Lucie can expect (assuming a 9% annual growth rate)

Think about it for a moment. Do you really think Lucie is going to grow up and **ONLY** contribute $1,000 per year into her retirement account? That is only $2.74 per day! That isn't going to happen. Especially not if I have anything to do with it!

If you only remember one thing in this book, make sure it is this!

The only way it is possible for you to become wealthy is to **pay your "FUTURE" self first!**

Before you pay a single bill; before you buy one article of clothing; before you buy a snack... take **15%** of what you make and immediately deposit it into your ROTH IRA!

Here is what I am talking about:

- You get a $300.00 pay check, $45.00 goes straight into your ROTH IRA
- You get $500.00 for your birthday, $75.00 goes straight into your ROTH IRA
- You have a yard sale and make $1,500.00, $225.00 goes straight into your ROTH IRA

After you do this, feel free to spend the rest of your money however you like!

Always pay your "FUTURE" self first!

Here's what I really love about paying your "FUTURE" self first:

1. By paying your "FUTURE" self first and depositing it directly into your ROTH IRA, you are forcing yourself to not only invest for your retirement, but you are forcing yourself to live on much less than you make **(especially if you get out of and/or stay out of debt!)**

2. **You will automatically increase the amount you save each and every time you get a raise or find new ways to make more money. This is crucial to creating Generational Wealth.**

   Most Americans try to figure out what they can buy when they start making more money. "Oh... I got a new job and I am making $30,000 more per year... awesome! Let's buy a bigger house, let's buy nicer cars, clothes, food, etc...."

   That's all well and good, but only if you decide to save and invest part of this new windfall of money... FIRST!

And here is the kicker for me... and I hope for you as well...

By saving **15%** of your take home pay, you will be living on much less than you make... So your money will be able to get to the point where it is making more money than you will be accustomed to living on... **this is the moment you will become wealthy!**

Check this out:

Let's assume Little Lucie reads this book and decides she is going to save and invest 15% of everything she makes, just like I am suggesting. Let's say she takes over the account at age 22, and her grandfather has invested $1,000.00 annually since the day she was born. And let's say she graduates from college and makes $50,000 per year her entire career (from the age of 22 to 65). And let's assume the S&P 500 grows an average of 9% per year... How much can little Lucie expect her retirement account to be worth the day she turns 65, assuming she invests 15% of her earnings her entire career? Are you ready for this?

$6,112,267.83!

As You Can See: $3,000,000 Is Peanuts Compared To This!

SETTING UP and FUNDING
YOUR ROTH IRA ACCOUNT

There are several rules that govern ROTH IRA accounts for minors.

For more detailed information and tutorial videos, go to **www.ButchMauldin.com**.

When and How To Buy SPY

OPTION 1:

If you can afford to deposit $1,000 or more directly into your ROTH IRA (or your newborn's ROTH IRA), then do it ASAP! And immediately buy as many shares as possible... and keep doing this every single year without fail....

OPTION 2:

Let's assume you can only save $25 per week. That's ok! Set it up to automatically make direct deposits into your ROTH IRA each and every week without fail... and the moment you have enough cash in your ROTH IRA to buy a share of SPY... do it immediately!

As of November 2021, the price of SPY is $452.25, so you could only purchase one share of SPY every 19 weeks. **That's okay... keep paying your "FUTURE" self first...that is the most important step of this entire process!** And simply buy a share every 19 weeks!

OPTION 3:

There are ways for you to purchase "Fractional Shares" as well.

For more information, go to www.ButchMauldin.com

And always remember, you are nothing but a buyer until the day you retire!

From now until the day you retire, all you need to do is:

- ✓ Pay your "FUTURE" self first; every single time you get paid

- ✓ Immediately deposit this amount directly into your ROTH IRA account

- ✓ Buy as many SPDRs (SPY) as you possibly can… as often as you possibly can

- ✓ Go live your life

That's it! Nothing Else.

- Don't worry about the bad news on TV
- Don't worry about the market going up too high
- Don't worry about the market going down too fast or for too long
- Don't worry about inflation, deflation or stagflation
- Don't worry about the next big thing everyone else is investing in

From now until the day you retire, **only worry about**:

- Spending as much time as possible with your friends and family
- Taking trips
- Donating your time to a good cause
- Reading a good book
- Taking flying lessons
- LIVING!

If you ever doubt this, go back and read Chapter 2!

Chapter 7

THE DAY YOU RETIRE

By the time you reach retirement age, you will have done nothing but buy SPDRs...

Month in, month out...

Year in, year out...

For decades...

By this moment in time, you will be on autopilot. I mean you will literally be able to:

- Pay your "FUTURE" self, first
- Deposit your money into your ROTH IRA
- Buy as many shares of SPY as often as possible...

In your sleep!

By this time, it will be so ingrained in you, that it will be very hard for you to stop.

But stop you must! Today is the day you've been waiting for!

Because today is the day you immediately:

- Stop Working
- Stop Saving
- Start Selling Your SPDRs

But you will keep on LIVING!

The moment you retire; you are nothing but a seller of SPDRs. But only sell what you need to live on each month so you can let the rest of your money keep growing inside your ROTH IRA

Let's assume that you read this book today and immediately start investing in SPDRs for the next 30 years, at which time you are ready, willing and able to retire. And this is what you have in your ROTH IRA:

Your ROTH IRA

➤	Years Invested	30
➤	Invested Per Year	$6,000.00
➤	Expected Average Annual Growth Rate:	8.59%
➤	Value of Your ROTH IRA at Retirement:	$757,813.46
➤	Amount You Can Expect to Pull Out Annually:	$65,000.00
➤	Amount You Can Expect to Live on Annually:	$65,000.00
➤	How Many Years You Expect to Live Past Retirement:	25 Years
➤	Total Amount You Expect to Pull Out After Retirement:	$1,625,000.00
➤	Expected Value of Your ROTH When You Pass Away:	$755,048.88
➤	Total Shares of SPDRs Owned	153

Let's jump into our imaginary time machine and go 30 years into the future:

So here it is, day 1 of your retirement and your ROTH IRA has a value of $755,048.88… all of which is invested in SPDRs.

If the value of SPDRs the first year you invested was $452.25 (value as of November 2021), and if this investment grew an average of 8.59% per year, then 30 years from now (Day 1 of retirement), each share of SPY will be worth $4,934.36 *(See Table 7, Next Page)*.

Table 7:

	Expected Value of One Share of SPDR at 8.59% Annual Growth			
Year	Beginning Value	Growth For the Year	Ending Value	Number of Shares Purchased
1	$452.25	$38.85	$491.10	12
2	$491.10	$42.19	$533.28	12
3	$533.28	$45.81	$579.09	12
4	$579.09	$49.74	$628.84	10
5	$628.84	$54.02	$682.85	10
6	$682.85	$58.66	$741.51	9
7	$741.51	$63.70	$805.21	8
8	$805.21	$69.17	$874.37	7
9	$874.37	$75.11	$949.48	7
10	$949.48	$81.56	$1,031.04	6
11	$1,031.04	$88.57	$1,119.61	6
12	$1,119.61	$96.17	$1,215.78	5
13	$1,215.78	$104.44	$1,320.22	5
14	$1,320.22	$113.41	$1,433.63	5
15	$1,433.63	$123.15	$1,556.78	4
16	$1,556.78	$133.73	$1,690.50	4
17	$1,690.50	$145.21	$1,835.72	3
18	$1,835.72	$157.69	$1,993.41	3
19	$1,993.41	$171.23	$2,164.64	3
20	$2,164.64	$185.94	$2,350.58	3
21	$2,350.58	$201.91	$2,552.50	3
22	$2,552.50	$219.26	$2,771.76	2
23	$2,771.76	$238.09	$3,009.85	2
24	$3,009.85	$258.55	$3,268.40	2
25	$3,268.40	$280.76	$3,549.15	2
26	$3,549.15	$304.87	$3,854.02	2
27	$3,854.02	$331.06	$4,185.08	2
28	$4,185.08	$359.50	$4,544.58	1
29	$4,544.58	$390.38	$4,934.96	2
30	$4,934.96	$423.91	$5,358.87	1
			Total Shares Owned	153

So now we know that 30 years from today… on Day 1 of your retirement… that your ROTH IRA has:

➢ 153 shares of SPY in it
➢ Each share of SPY is now worth $4,934.36
➢ The total value of your ROTH IRA account is $755,048.88 (153 x $4,934.36)

- Each share of SPY can be expected to grow by $423.91 this year (this is an estimate)
- Which means your 153 shares of SPY are expected to make you $64,858.23… this year

TIME TO RETIRE!

...Which Means It Is Time to Start Selling Some Shares!

But not all at once…

Remember, it is compound growth that got you to this point and it will be compound growth that carries you all the way to the finish line…

AND I MEAN THAT LITERALLY

Don't forget… this investment needs to continue compounding until the very day you die!

In order to do that, you need to sell as few shares as possible in order to pull out the $65,000 per year you need to live on for the next 20-30 years!

So, simple math will tell you how many shares you need to sell. So, let's get to it:

Step 1: Sell Enough Shares To Live On Each Month

$65,000 Per Year / 12 Months = $5,416.67 Per Month

Step 2: Figure Out How Many Shares You Need To Sell This Month

Current price of SPY is: $4,934.36 and you want $5,416.67 for this month. You can choose to sell 1 or 2 shares of SPY.

Step 3: Go Live Your Life and Repeat This Process Again In 30 Days

Do these three steps the rest of your life! That's it!

Wait a second! If I sell one share per month, I am going to run out of money in less than 13 years!

Great question! Glad you asked.

Don't forget, you are expecting your shares of SPY to continue growing in value at an annual average of 8.59%. As the values grow, you can expect to sell fewer and fewer shares each year in order to raise the $65,000.00 per year to live on. As you can see in the table below, this is what the price of each share of SPDR is expected to be for the next 25 years of your retirement:

Table 8: Expected Value of a Share of SPY for the Next 25 Years

	Expected Value of One Share of SPDR at 8.59% Annual Growth				
Age	Beginning Value	Growth For the Year	Ending Value	Number of Shares Sold	Money to Live On
66	$5,358.87	$460.33	$5,819.20	12	$64,306.44
67	$5,819.20	$499.87	$6,319.07	11	$64,011.17
68	$6,319.07	$542.81	$6,861.87	10	$63,190.66
69	$6,861.87	$589.43	$7,451.31	9	$61,756.86
70	$7,451.31	$640.07	$8,091.38	9	$67,061.78
71	$8,091.38	$695.05	$8,786.43	8	$64,731.01
72	$8,786.43	$754.75	$9,541.18	7	$61,504.98
73	$9,541.18	$819.59	$10,360.77	7	$66,788.25
74	$10,360.77	$889.99	$11,250.76	6	$62,164.60
75	$11,250.76	$966.44	$12,217.20	6	$67,504.54
76	$12,217.20	$1,049.46	$13,266.65	5	$61,081.98
77	$13,266.65	$1,139.61	$14,406.26	5	$66,333.27
78	$14,406.26	$1,237.50	$15,643.76	4	$57,625.04
79	$15,643.76	$1,343.80	$16,987.56	4	$62,575.03
80	$16,987.56	$1,459.23	$18,446.79	4	$67,950.22
81	$18,446.79	$1,584.58	$20,031.37	3	$55,340.36
82	$20,031.37	$1,720.69	$21,752.06	3	$60,094.10
83	$21,752.06	$1,868.50	$23,620.56	3	$65,256.18
84	$23,620.56	$2,029.01	$25,649.57	3	$70,861.68
85	$25,649.57	$2,203.30	$27,852.87	3	$76,948.70
86	$27,852.87	$2,392.56	$30,245.43	2	$55,705.73
87	$30,245.43	$2,598.08	$32,843.51	2	$60,490.85
88	$32,843.51	$2,821.26	$35,664.77	2	$65,687.02
89	$35,664.77	$3,063.60	$38,728.37	2	$71,329.54
90	$38,728.37	$3,326.77	$42,055.14	2	$77,456.74
		Shares Remaining		21	$1,617,760.72
		Value of Shares		$813,295.77	

As you can see, the price per share will determine how many shares you will need to sell. At the age of 66, you can expect to need to sell 12 shares of SPY to raise the $65,000 you will need to live on for that year. By the time you are 86, this number will drop all the way down to 2 shares.

Looking at Table 8, you should expect to have 21 shares of SPY remaining in your ROTH IRA 25 years after you retire and expect to pass away... and those shares will be worth approximately $813,295.77 (21 shares x $38,728.37 per share)... and that is after you will have been able to sell $1,617,760.72 worth of shares to live on TAX FREE!

In short, you can expect to be able to live on approximately $65,000 per year for the rest of your life and be able to leave approximately $813,000 to your loved ones after you pass away.

That's the magic of compound growth! The previous page may be a little difficult to get your head around. Don't worry about it. All you need to do is simply sell as few shares as you need to live on... that's it!

Remember, 8.59% is just an estimate of what the expected average annual growth rate of what SPY will be. The actual results will be completely different... **especially on a year-by-year basis. Remember, the market could go up, it could go down or it could go sideways. There will be times during your retirement that the market will go up several years in a row and times the market will go down several years in a row. The previous examples were for educational purposes and I chose to keep the growth rate consistent in order to make it easier for me to explain those concepts to you.

On the next page, I am going to show you my strategy for withdrawing money from my retirement account once I reach retirement age in 2037.

MY WITHDRAWAL PLAN

Let's pretend it is 2037 and I have just retired. Below is my ROTH IRA. Unfortunately, I didn't hit the jackpot, because my parents didn't get a chance to read this book when I was an infant. That's okay, because I was still able to build myself a little nest egg.

My ROTH IRA

➢ Years Invested	30
➢ Invested Per Year	$6,000.00
➢ Expected Average Annual Growth Rate:	8.59%
➢ Value of Your ROTH IRA at Retirement:	$757,813.46
➢ Amount You Can Expect to Pull Out Annually:	$65,000.00
➢ Amount You Can Expect to Live on Annually:	$65,000.00
➢ How Many Years You Expect to Live Past Retirement:	25 Years
➢ Total Amount You Expect to Pull Out After Retirement:	$1,625,000.00
➢ Expected Value of Your ROTH When You Pass Away:	$755,048.88
➢ Total Shares of SPDRs Owned	153
➢ What I Need to Live on For a Given Year	$45,000.00

EXAMPLE 1:

On the first day of my retirement, I am going to look at how much my ROTH IRA grew over the past 12 months. If it grew by more than $65,000, then I will pull out the full $65,000 and use that money to live on for the next 12 months.

EXAMPLE 2:

If my ROTH IRA grew by $45,000-$64,000 in the previous 12 months, I will pull that amount out to live on for the next 12 months.

EXAMPLE 3:

If my ROTH grew by less than $45,000 in the previous 12 months, I will pull out $45,000 to live on.

My Decision Tree

Growth Rate of My ROTH	I Will Pull Out:
$95,000	$65,000
$75,000	$65,000
$68,000	$65,000
$63,000	$63,000
$58,000	$58,000
$19,000	$45,000
($50,000)	$45,000
($130,000)	$45,000

A couple of points I would like to make about this plan:

1. No matter how much my ROTH IRA grows in a given year, I will not take more out than I planned on prior to retiring (in this example it was $65,000). I want to sell as **FEW** shares as possible, because I have no interest in killing the golden goose (my shares in SPY).

2.   The reason I will sell enough shares to cover my living expenses for an entire year (all at one time) is because I have no clue what the market will do in the next 12 months. I had rather take my money out of the market and not worry about it until it is time to withdraw more cash a year down the road.

3.   When the market drops, I will sell the minimum number of shares possible for me to live on. In this example, $45,000 is the amount.

This selling strategy is simple and fits my personality.

At the end of the day, there are so many options for you to consider when it comes to determining exactly how much you will sell and when.

This is one topic that I highly suggest you dig into and research as you get closer to retirement.

Just remember that the only thing that matters is to not run out of money! That is simply not an option for you in your eighties or nineties!

Most every financial advisor (which I am not) will tell you to move 40% of your money into bonds as you get closer to retirement. I am not saying they are wrong, but I am saying it isn't what I am going to do.

I firmly believe the S&P 500 is the safest bet on the planet; and I also believe it will give me the highest return on my money, which is crucial. But I want to be clear... this is MY decision based on my personality, knowledge and opinions.

Now that you have nearly completed this book, you need to make your own decisions based on your knowledge, personality and opinions.

Purchasing nothing but SPY's for the rest of your life may not be something you want to do… **don't do it if that is the case.** Remember, this is YOUR life and YOUR money. Do what is best for you!

Whether you choose to follow the plan I have outlined in this book or not, I sincerely hope you have learned something useful and can apply to help build a legacy, create **GENERATIONAL WEALTH** and change your family tree.

I would love to hear what your plans are moving forward, different ideas you are considering and milestones you hit along the journey of your life.

Please go to **www.ButchMauldin.com**, bookmark the page and stay in touch! I am rooting for you!

Now, Let's Take Just A Few More Minutes To Envision Your Legacy!

Chapter 8

LET'S ENVISION YOUR LEGACY

I want you to imagine this with me. A few years from now, a new baby is born into your family. His name is Billy and he is your grandson! And because you read this book, you made the decision to set up a ROTH IRA in his name, deposit $1,000 into his account and invest all of it in **SPY**.

Not only that, you bought this book for Billy's other grandparents and after reading it, they decided they wanted to contribute $1,000 per year... **just like you!**

So, here is little Billy... not even able to crawl yet and he has a retirement account with $2,000 per year being invested in it!

As the next 10 years roll by, all you do is enjoy your grandson's company. You take him to the ballgame, to Disney World, to the beach... you live life! But what little Billy doesn't know is that you and his other grandparents have quietly contributed a total of $20,000 into his retirement account... and it was easy!

On his 10th birthday, you decide to take a peek at his account to see what it is worth. You know it doesn't matter, because that account has 55 more years to compound for him. But you take a peek any way and see it is now worth $28,550.27. It's not currently growing at an average rate of 9% like that idiotic author told you to expect it to be when you read that book a few years ago, but you start thinking to yourself, 'Wow, my grandson's money has made him $8,550.27 and he can't even drive yet!'

You smile, log out of the account and start driving to your grandson's birthday party. You don't speak a word about this account. You just go in, put on a party hat, sing "Happy Birthday" to little Billy, eat some cake and ice cream... You just live!

A few years later, you decide it is time to dust off that book you read a few years ago, re-read a few chapters and login to **www.ButchMauldin.com** to go over some video lessons before heading over to see your grandson. And for the first time in Billy's life, he starts learning about the concept of "Paying His FUTURE Self First" and why you want him to always take 15% and invest it.

Shortly after this conversation, Billy's mom and dad decide it is time for him to start getting an allowance. They are going to pay him $20 per week to clean his room, take out the trash and load up the dishwasher. And Billy has agreed to save 15% of his money just like you taught him. So, for 3 years, Billy gives you $3.50 per week to invest for him.

Little Billy is building good habits at a very young age!

As the years tick away, you and his other grandparents continue to contribute $2,000 per year into Billy's account. In the blink of an eye, Billy is turning 16 years old! As you head out to his birthday party, you look at his retirement account to see how much it is valued at today. You know it doesn't matter, because that account still has nearly 50 years to compound, but you just can't help yourself. You log onto the account and it is valued at $59,400. You think about that idiotic author of that book you read years ago... The S&P still isn't averaging 9% like he said to expect... But then you say to yourself...

"Wow! Billy has more money in his retirement account than most 30-year-olds and he doesn't even know it! I can't wait to tell him... It won't be long now!"

You head out to the birthday party and enjoy the day! At the party, Billy tells you he is starting a job next week. He will be working at a grocery store and he will be making $15 per hour and he plans on working 20 hours a week. So, he will be giving you $40 per week to invest for him... just like you have been doing for the past three years.

You are so excited, because you now realize that Billy naturally increased his savings the moment he got a raise! He didn't have to make a hard decision like you did. It wasn't even a choice! Your grandson has been bred to become wealthy!

You decide that it is time to dust off that old book and have Billy read it. You know he is more than capable of understanding the concepts in the book. After a few hours, Billy is finished with the book, and for the first time you get to show your grandson his retirement account! The one that you have been contributing to for the past 16 years. And you get to show him that everything he just read in that old book is true and the $59,400 balance in his account proves it.

Just imagine the look on your grandson's face! Just stop and consider this life altering moment! Just think about how the abstract things he had just read about in that dusty old book becoming his new reality in the blink of an eye... **just imagine!**

Then you explain to Billy that you and his other grandparents will continue contributing $2,000 per year until he gets out of college, as long as he agrees to contribute 15% of his income from his new job at the grocery store and you ask him to go to **www.ButchMauldin.com** so he can watch some video tutorials that will help him to better understand the concepts in the book that he just read.

For the next 6 years, Billy works at that grocery store... and just like he said, he gives you $40 every single week ($2,080.00 per year) without fail so you can invest it for him in *HIS* ROTH IRA. And he does this until the day he graduates from college.

Prior to leaving for Billy's college graduation, you decide to take a look at his retirement account one last time. Of course, it doesn't matter, because that account still has more than 40 years to compound... but you just can't help yourself. You log onto and see that it is now valued at $125,452.26.

You do some quick math and you grumble to yourself about that silly author telling you to expect a 9% return... it hasn't averaged 9% at any point in the past 22 years. But you smile and say to yourself, "Wow! Billy really hit the jackpot!"

You think about the measly $1,000 that you contributed each year for the past twenty-two years and you know that you didn't miss one penny of that money. And you know whatever you had spent that money on would most likely be long gone... not even a memory.

As you are driving to Billy's graduation, you give him a call. You ask him if he is ready to take over his retirement account.

He answers with a confident, **"Of course I am. You had me read that book, I have watched every video lesson at www.ButchMauldin.com and I have been watching you invest in nothing but the S&P 500 for the past 6 years. It is simple. A 10th grader could do it. Wow. I can't believe I am graduating college today and my retirement account is valued at $125,000! Thank you so much! I love you and I will see you at graduation!"**

A few hours later, you get to watch Billy graduate with a music degree. He has already landed his dream job as the band instructor for his old middle school. It is the only job he has ever wanted... and he made it happen. He would have taken the job for free...that's how much he loves it. It's a small-town middle school and they can only afford to pay Billy $38,000 per year. Billy is happy with that... money doesn't really motivate him... music does!

So, for the next 20 years, Billy "Pays His FUTURE Self First" and invests $475 per month into his retirement account just like you taught him. **He doesn't even think about it. It is as natural as breathing for him... because it is all he has ever known.**

And during those years, he starts a ROTH IRA for his newborn daughter and contributes $1,000 per year into it. And just like you did with him, he teaches her the concept of "Paying Her FUTURE Self First" at a very young age.

After 20 years, Billy's job vanishes. The old school has been shut down because it is in awful shape and the county has decided to combine two schools. Billy was offered the job at the new school, but he knew the other band instructor would be let go and he simply couldn't allow that to happen.

He calls to let you know he is going to work at the local coffee shop. It's a little less pay... $29,000 per year, but they said he and his jazz band are welcome to play there every Friday night... that's really why he is taking the job.

He also tells you that his retirement account is now up to $1 million dollars for the first time ever.

You are not surprised, but it still stuns you.

Billy also tells you that your 14-year-old granddaughter's retirement account is now valued at $42,450.00 and that he has just started to give her an allowance and has been teaching her to save 15% of what she makes, just like you taught him when he was a little boy...

Your Legacy is Growing!

Billy ends up working at that coffee shop until he decides to retire at the age of 65. He could have retired 15 years ago, but he loved what he was doing. And of course, Billy continued "Paying His FUTURE Self First" and investing $362.50 per month (15% of his pay) just like you taught him many years ago.

On the day Billy retires, he looks at the value of his account that you set up for him 65 years ago. Today it is worth $3,150,254.45. And because he is your grandson and you taught him well... he runs the math and realizes that the S&P 500 has only grown at an average rate of 6.80%.... and he thinks to himself... '9%... what in the world was that author thinking when he wrote that book?!'

Billy decides he can pull out $210,000 per year to live on...tax free! Which is 8 times more than he is used to living on. He has no clue what to do with all of that money, but he knows he will have fun figuring it out.

Then Billy's thoughts turn to the one and only person he wants to talk to...

So, he jumps in the car and drives to the cemetery to tell you the great news.

He looks down at your grave site, thinks about all the special memories you both shared together. He kneels down and says, "Thank you so much for all you did for me. I am so lucky to be your grandson... **Little Lucie isn't the only one who hit the jackpot!"**

This is your legacy! Now go make it happen!

At the end of the day, what I really want to leave you with is this... Do not worry about what the market does over the next 40 years. It will go up and it will go down and it will go sideways. Always remember this... every single person in this country wants the market to go up... CEOs of these publicly traded companies, politicians, presidents, school teachers... everyone. And when you purchase these SPY shares... not only are you putting your money to work for you... But you are putting every politician... every President and every CEO of these publicly-traded companies to work for you, too!

The simple fact is, you are putting the full force and weight of the American economy to work for you... **all while you sleep well at night.**

Now, go change your financial future, create generational wealth for your children and your children's children... and please make sure to tell everyone you know about this book!

Sincerely,
Butch Mauldin

To the Love of My Life, Kelli Mauldin
Let's Share All the Love and Laughter That a Lifetime Will Allow!
-George Strait

Made in the USA
Coppell, TX
21 January 2022

72030356R00059